T0301228

MIXED IN MINUTES

MIXED IN MINUTES

50 QUICK & EASY COCKTAILS TO MAKE AT HOME

DAN WHITESIDE

SPHERE

SPHERE

First published in Great Britain in 2021 by Sphere
Copyright © Dan Whiteside, 2021
Photography: Sam Folan
Design concept: Dan Whiteside
Book Design: Rob Hearn
Cover illustration: Trevor May

3 5 7 9 10 8 6 4 2

A CIP catalogue record for this book is available from the
British Library.
ISBN 978-0-7515-8375-5
Printed and bound in Great Britain by Bell and Bain Ltd, Glasgow
Papers used by Little, Brown are from well-managed forests
and other responsible sources.

MIX
Paper from
responsible sources
FSC® C104740

Sphere
An imprint of
Little, Brown Book Group
Carmelite House
50 Victoria Embankment
London EC4Y 0DZ

An Hachette UK Company
www.hachette.co.uk

www.littlebrown.co.uk

CONTENTS

INTRODUCTION

DRINKS AT HOME

More than ever, people want to host friends and family in their homes. Entertaining at home is all about enjoying the moment, making memories and building relationships, so I wanted to put a cocktail book together that allows people to make delicious cocktails without taking their time away from the important things in life.

Until recently I had no intentions of publishing a book. I've worked in the drinks industry for over 20 years in some of the UK's best bars, but it's only been during the COVID-19 lockdown that I realised that I took having a nice drink at home for granted. Friends and family were mostly put off making cocktails at home because they didn't even know where to start, but seeing what I could easily achieve at home with no cocktail equipment, and how simple it was opened their eyes – they couldn't believe how easy it was. Seeing them experiment and make their own gave me the idea. People had been stuck at home, and after a post-lockdown barbecue they were inspired to make cocktails themselves.

Being a father to a five-year-old and spending most weekends at friends' barbecues, birthday parties, nursery gatherings and the like, I saw the difference between the drink experience when in my home and when it was our turn to be hosted! A gathering at ours would regularly turn into a cocktail session after the food had been devoured. Piña Coladas, Daiquiris and Negronis are the norm, and with a little bit of thought and preparation, cocktails for a small gathering are incredibly simple and basically on tap. When we would go to a friend's house, wine, beer and Prosecco would be about it.

Here was the idea: strip away all the information that people don't need so that they can make simple, consistent, delicious cocktails, without cocktail-making equipment or complicated techniques, all mixed in minutes.

I've taken 50 classic and contemporary cocktails that you can make easily at home, and I've included options for seasonally twisting your drink.

Each chapter takes you through some of my favourite cocktails, but more importantly *your* favourite cocktails, using methods that you can actually do at home, so there's no fancy cocktail equipment required. I wanted to debunk the myths around cocktails: that you can never make a cocktail as good as the ones you drink in a bar; how it's too difficult to get them consistent; and how they're too expensive to make. There is also a belief that experience is needed, and that only qualified mixologists with years of training can produce and twist great drinks, with months spent on the development of new drinks. This is not the case. Twisting your favourite drink by swapping out its building blocks with a different flavour is simple, and it's as easy as thinking of your favourite flavours.

For most recipes I've also included options for spritzing or 'lengthening' your drink, to halve its alcohol content. I recommend different flavoured tonics and sodas to pair with each cocktail, making them more refreshing and accessible, and less boozy. Over the last few years, there has been a huge lean towards people wanting lower and zero alcoholic drinks. Forget sugary mocktails, these are serious alternatives for drinking less alcohol. People are deciding to drink less for all sorts of reasons, including mental health, fitness, calorie intake and not having to deal with five-year-olds when you have a hangover!

You'll also find some simple highball (spirit and mixer) drink recipes at the end of each spirit section, including tequila and tonic, vodka and soda – and even great twists on the humble G&T.

Almost all the ingredients can be found in your local supermarket, if not online, and you won't need to buy any unusual liqueurs, tinctures or bottles that are only going to collect dust on your kitchen shelves and waste your money.

I'll show you how you can create consistently delicious drinks in just a few minutes, and how to make them look amazing.

The most important thing is that you have fun and get to drink amazing drinks at home!

Time to demystify cocktail making – let's get started,

Dan Whiteside

HOW TO USE THIS BOOK

Every drink is about balance:
• Sweet vs sour
• Strong vs dilute
• Wet vs dry
• Flavours

All the recipes in this book are put together using my taste and experience, but everyone has a different palate and taste preference. If you prefer your Daiquiri sweeter, add more sugar. If you prefer your Mojito a touch more tart, add less sugar – simple.

If you don't have the correct alcohol you need to make a cocktail – say, for example, you happen to have vodka but you want to make a Daiquiri (which uses white rum) – give the different alcohol a try. It won't be a standard Daiquiri, but it will still taste great. If you have gin in your cupboard and you want to make a Mojito (which also uses white rum), mix it up. It won't be a traditional Mojito, but again it will taste great – you get the idea?

A trick I learnt years ago was to taste the drink with a bar spoon, teaspoon or straw before mixing or shaking. This way I could taste the balance of the drink before finishing it off. If it tastes great before you shake, it will taste even better afterwards! Once you've shaken or mixed and poured it into a glass, it's generally too late to fix.

Shaking, mixing or blending does three things to a drink:
• It mixes the ingredients together.
• It chills the drink down.
• It adds dilution.

Every single cocktail needs these three components: everyone wants their cocktail mixed together; everyone wants their cocktail nice and cold (besides hot cocktails); and everyone wants dilution to take the edge off the alcohol and bring balance to the drink. For example, an Old Fashioned is pretty much straight whiskey with a touch of sugar, but without the dilution it would just burn. By being chilled and diluted, the ingredients become more accessible and they open the whisky up so that you can enjoy the flavours.

♢ TWIST

Each cocktail has an idea to twist: to add different flavours. By far the best way is to change up the sugar syrup; for example, swap the sugar syrup in a Daiquiri for a strawberry syrup – delicious and simple. Can you throw a handful of strawberries in with sugar and water? Yes you can!

Alternatively, you can just add the fruit straight to your ingredients before blending them, but the pulp will give the drink more of a smoothie consistency than a standard cocktail.

GARNISHES

All cocktails have their preferred garnish that complements the drink: an orange twist with a Negroni, mint with a Mojito – but this book is all about simplicity. If you have berries, or a different citrus fruit that matches the flavour, add these anyway. They will still make the drink look great and will complement the flavours, so give it a try.

For almost all drinks, the garnish is placed at the edge (rim) of the drink. This gives you the opposite side of the glass to drink from, and if using a straw, the garnish will be next to it, meaning that you get the aroma of the garnish while drinking.

SPRITZING

Most cocktails in this book have a recommendation on how to spritz – or lengthen, or top up – using different mixers. Generally, spritzing is associated with Aperol or a wine spritz, but adding an effervescent mixer can be applied to most cocktails. The main reason for spritzing cocktails is to bring down the alcohol content (ABV) of the drink, which makes it more accessible and palatable, and it means that your cocktail is longer and more refreshing. Instead of having straight-up Negronis in the afternoon, mix them with Mediterranean Tonic and keep everyone standing up for longer.

- When you make a blended cocktail, pour half the drink into a highball or wine glass, fill with ice and top with a mixer. If the drink contains egg white, such as a Sour, leave this out.
- When you make a 'built' cocktail, simply halve the ingredients and add them to the glass, fill with ice and top with the mixer.
- For a shorter drink such as an Old Fashioned or Negroni, you can use a shorter glass such as a rocks glass.
- For a drink that already has a mixer such as a Collins or Aperol Spritz, simply halve the non-fizzy ingredients and top with the spritzer.

Remember that the recommendations are exactly that: play around with different mixers to your taste.

HIGHBALLS

A highball is a mixed alcoholic drink comprised of a measure of alcohol and a larger proportion of mixer: think G&T, vodka and soda, or rum and ginger beer. Besides the G&T, highballs are often forgotten about at home, and yet they can produce simple and delicious drinks. Some even go as far as to be classified as cocktails.

Beyond the cocktail recipes in this book, you will find some great alternatives to the usual highball drinks, taking the five main spirits you might find at home and giving them a twist. You'll find these at the end of each spirit section. For each of these spirits, there are recommendations based on what will work best, but, as with the rest of the book, try whatever you wish!

TOOLS

Spoon A cocktail spoon is ideal, but if you don't have a long spoon, you could use a metal straw or even a chopstick. Use this to stir an Old Fashioned or a jug of Cava Sangria.

NutriBullet or bullet-style blender to blend any cocktails instead of shaking.

Measures If you don't have a liquid measure, you can use digital scales to measure accurately how much your measuring device can hold and to measure the amount of ice you need. Here's how:
1. Put your container on the scales and set it to zero.
2. Change the measuring unit to ml.
3. Pour in your ingredients, and the scales will measure what you add; for example, 50ml rum + 30ml lime juice + 25ml sugar syrup = 105ml. Don't worry if you are a few ml out.
4. Add the ice and blend!

Jug A metal or glass jug for mixing pitchers of Cava Sangria. Metal jugs work best, because they keep your drink colder for longer.

Spirit measure/jigger A double-ended measure is a great tool to have (and costs £5ish), because it lets you measure 15/25/35/50ml. If you can't find one, and you don't have digital scales, try the following:
• Egg cup – these generally hold 50ml
• Ice-cream scoop – these generally hold 25ml and are easy to use without spilling
• Shot glass – generally 50ml
• Tablespoon – 15ml
• Teaspoon – 5ml
• Measuring spoons

For ease, I've included a conversion guide on page 126 to use if you have a different kind of measuring tool.

General kitchen tools Saucepans, a sharp knife, chopping board, empty glass bottles (empty clean wine or beer bottles work great), perhaps a carafe or jug.

GLASSWARE

Your cocktail will look great in a nice coupe, flute or highball, but if you don't have these can you drink from a tumbler? Of course!

| Coupe/ coupette | Collins/ highball | Rocks/ tumbler | Martini | Flute | Wine glass |

METHODS

In this book there are only three simple methods: blend, build and small batch. No muddling, shaking, throwing, layering, or straining.

Build is basically adding all the ingredients to the glass, filling with ice and giving it a quick stir.

Blending is my substitute for shaking. Shaking usually smashes the ingredients together, chills and dilutes. With the right amount of ice, blending does the same job.

Also, a higher percentage of homes are going to have small blenders, such as NutriBullets, rather than cocktail shakers. Blending gets a consistent result, with zero wastage of ice and less mess. The perfect blend is with 45g ice, or about 4 small ice cubes. (Note that blades can be 'dulled' over time by ice, but this is more likely if you blend ice only. Adding liquid to the mix helps the process of the ice being broken down.)

Small batch (Martini, Martinez or Manhattan) is a simpler and more consistent alternative to stirring in a mixing glass. Stirring your drink this way with ice simply chills your ingredients, mixes them and dilutes them, like a gentler version of shaking. The problem with stirring is that you need a mixing vessel, something to stir with, and lots of ice that will only be wasted afterwards. With batching, all you need to do is pre-chill your ingredients, add the correct amount of chilled dilution and you're ready. Similar to the sweet/sour balance, you might prefer your drink with more or less dilution, to your taste.

PREPARATION

Although some of your cocktail basics need to be prepared in advance, they are all very simple and will take you just a few minutes to make.

SUGAR SYRUP

Sugar syrup is melted sugar and water, and is a simple, consistent and easily mixable way of getting sweetness into your drink – you don't want crunchy grains of sugar in your Mojito waiting to dissolve.

The recipe just requires equal parts of caster sugar and water. My usual recipe, which is enough for multiple drinks, is as follows.

200g caster sugar
200ml water

1. In a saucepan warm the sugar and water over a high heat, stirring occasionally until the sugar has melted and the liquid is clear. This should take only 5 minutes. (Alternatively, you can microwave for 90 seconds, give it a stir, and then another 90 seconds should do it.)
2. Cool and transfer to a bottle and keep in the fridge.

As there is a small amount of evaporation, this recipe should result in about 300ml of syrup.

A key part of this book is giving you simple flavour-twist ideas, and the best way is to flavour your sugar syrup with fruit. This way, your drink has exactly the same process. You can use fresh or frozen fruits (which are also usually pre-cut). Below are some ideas to flavour your syrup using the above recipe.
• 100g raspberries or blackberries
• 100g strawberries, sliced
• 100g grapefruit segments
• 100g pineapple chunks, no skin
• 100g watermelon, no skin
• 1 vanilla pod, sliced open lengthways
• 2 mint sprigs, stalks included
• 1 small red chilli, sliced in half (washed and deseeded)
• Honey (equal parts honey and water)
• Honey and ginger, equal parts honey and water, 1 large slice of fresh ginger, peeled

Add the flavouring to the sugar syrup recipe as it warms; it will impart a lovely colour and flavour. Leave the fruit or flavouring in the syrup as it cools, then remove it before bottling. Easy!

PEACH PURÉE *(for Cava Sangria, page 109 and Bellini, page 105)*

400g tin of peaches, in juice
85ml sugar syrup

1. Blend both ingredients for 10-15 seconds until smooth. Store in the fridge.

NOTE: other fruit purées can be simple enough to make at home, but will require a different recipe due to different levels of acidity. They can also be shop-bought.

CREAM OF COCONUT *(for Piña Colada, page 31)*

Coco Lopez is the perfect ingredient for a Piña Colada, but this can be difficult to find, so we'll make our own. This recipe will make 8 Piña Coladas, so scale up or down depending on your needs.

200ml coconut cream
200g caster sugar
1 pinch sea salt

1. Warm all the ingredients in a saucepan until the sugar is dissolved and the mixture is smooth.
2. Cool and store in the fridge.

CITRUS FRUIT JUICE

Fresh is always best. You can get away with most supermarket lemon juice for a Sour or Collins, but stay away from lime juice: it tastes like cordial.

Before cutting limes or lemons, give them a gentle roll under the palm of your hand on a hard surface. This softens the fruit, making it easier to juice.

For juicing, cut down the middle widthways and squeeze against the side of a cup or bowl if you do not have a juicer. A Mexican Elbow is the best tool, which you can find online and from most large supermarkets for about £6.

Fresh lemon and lime juice can last 2-3 days if kept sealed and chilled. If you know you will be making multiple cocktails, squeeze enough in advance and pour into a container - glass bottles work best. Keep in the fridge.

EGG

Eggs are a common ingredient in cocktails, from egg white in a Sour or a Fizz to whole egg in a Flip. As used in these recipes, egg white adds viscosity and mouthfeel, and it binds the ingredients together, creating a wonderfully smooth, foamy drink.

Vegan alternatives such as aquafaba (chickpea water) and Ms. Better's Foamer also work great.

ICE

Simply put, ice is your best friend and should be thought of as a key ingredient. The ice in your drink should never float; it should be packed in the glass. The more ice, the colder and better tasting your drink will be, and as it slowly melts it adds the much-needed dilution to your drink.

Ice balls and blocks melt a lot slower than regular-sized ice cubes due to their density, keeping your drink fresher for longer. If you are making a jug of my Aperol Spritz, Cava Sangria, or even an Old Fashioned, using an ice block or ball will keep your drink colder for longer without melting into a watery mess. They also look great, and your friends will definitely be impressed.

Blocks To make ice blocks, fill a Tupperware/plastic container with water and place in your freezer. When ready to use, simply smash the ice into large chunks. The easiest way is to score lines on the ice with a sharp knife, then stick the knife point in the line and whack!

Balls To make balls, simply fill balloons with water to the desired size, and gently place them in the freezer. When ready, peel off the balloon and give the ice a quick rinse with cold water.

Cubes If you know you will need lots of cubed ice for a gathering, make the ice cubes and bag them up over a few days. I'm lucky enough to have a banging fridge with an ice machine. I empty this into food bags and keep in the freezer the day before; that way the ice machine will be full again on the day of the party leaving me with double the amount of ice. If you have ice trays, you can use the same method.

FREEZING FRUIT

When using large tropical fruits such as pineapple or melon, the best thing to do is to chop up the whole fruit, put it into a container and stick it in the freezer. This way you will have no waste, and you will have ice-cold fruit ready for use whenever you need it – and it'll last for ages. Also, if blending fruit directly into a drink such as a Piña Colada, frozen fruit works so much better. Whenever I buy a pineapple I pick and freeze the leaves; they are great as garnishes and keep for ever in the freezer.

 BATCHING

Batching is simply a way of preparing larger amounts of your drinks in advance; think, a bottle of premade Old Fashioned, ready to pour at will, or a large jug of Aperol Spritz to share – or not!

For a strong, spirit-based cocktail, such an Old Fashioned or Negroni, simply divide the bottle or container size (clean wine bottles work best) by the amount of liquid in the cocktail recipe; for example:

750ml wine bottle
75ml Negroni (page 73)
750ml @ 75ml each = 10 cocktails

Just to be safe, I would go with nine cocktails, which for a Negroni is as simple as:

225ml Campari
225ml sweet vermouth
225ml gin

For a drink served straight up, such as the Martini, include the dilution (chilled water) to the bottle; for example:

750ml wine bottle
105ml Martini (pages 37, 39, 43) including the 20ml dilution
735ml/105ml = 7 cocktails

Pop the cap on and leave it in the fridge ready to pour. A spirit-based drink can be left for months with little effect. The flavour won't really change, unlike one aged in a wooden barrel, but if left for long enough the flavours can settle and become smoother.

Something I like to do at home is infuse the whole cocktail. With the above recipe, for example, you have a bit of room left in the bottle (because the mixture makes a bit less than 750ml), so try adding a handful of sliced strawberries or raspberries directly to the bottle. Remove the fruit by straining after 24–48 hours, and your cocktail will have a wonderful hint of fresh fruit.

With other drinks such as Aperol Spritz, or even a Mojito, you can batch into a large jug for multiple drinks.

Again, work out how many you can fit into the jug; add all the ingredients and keep in the fridge just before a party. Add a ball or block of ice before you serve.

DECORATING A DRINK

An amazing way to add colour, flavour and instant Instagram likes to your drinks is by using different garnishes.

🖌 FRESH GARNISHES

- Lemon wedges – cut the fruit lengthways in half, the cut each half into half, and half again. Unless instructed otherwise, garnishes should be placed together in the top of the drink, by the rim. If using a straw, place the garnish and straw next to each other.
- Lime wedges – cut the fruit lengthways in half, cut each half into thirds.
- Wheels – starting at the top or bottom, simply cut slices straight down.
- Cucumber slices – cut at a 45-degree angle for a nice long slice.
- Edible flowers – as flowers don't last more than a few days, freeze them for future use, but leave the lid off the container because the trapped moisture will ruin the flowers as they freeze.

✳ DRIED GARNISHES

You can easily find many dried garnishes online, including:

Freeze-dried fruit Health food shops and online retailers sell these. Honeyberry do a great range. Sprinkling a pinch of fruit powder on top of a Sour, Piña Colada, or G&T gives a pop of colour like a splash of bright paint, and the flavour will complement.

Edible rice paper Available online. Add any design or photo you want onto an edible disc, and then onto your drink. This works especially well in a foamy drink such as a Sour or a Piña Colada; the disc melts into the foam leaving just the design on your cocktail. Think photos of your partner for his/her birthday, or a company logo for a product launch: the opportunities are literally endless.

Dried edible flower petals Uncle Roy's do a great colourful range, available online from about £6–7 per jar; they will last forever, too!

Dehydrated fruit This can be a nice way to give a simple fruit a different look and texture, and it is longer lasting. I actually have a dehydrator at home and often use apples, citrus fruits, pineapple and even strawberries. Try experimenting with different heats and times, using your oven; this should start you off:

1. Heat your oven to its lowest setting with the fan on.
2. Put thinly sliced fruit of your choice on baking paper on a baking tray.
3. Put into the oven and leave for 6–10 hours, turning every hour or so. The fruit should be thin, slightly crispy and full of colour.

TYPES OF COCKTAILS

When you begin making different cocktails, you'll quickly find that they start feeling familiar to each other. There are different types, or families, but generally all have a connection. Most cocktails are only one or two ingredients different from the next. I have simplified the many different types of families of cocktails below.

Collins: Tom, John
Spirit/Sour/Sweet/
Soda

Sour: Whiskey Sour,
Margarita, Daiquiri
Spirit/Sour/Sweet/Egg
white (optional)

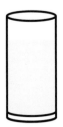

Highball: Gin & Tonic
Spirit/Carbonated
mixer

Colada: Piña Colada
Spirit/Sweet/Fruit

Spirit forward:
Old Fashioned
Spirit/Sweet (optional)
Bitters

Aperitivo: Negroni,
Aperol Spritz,
Americano
(A family of pre-dinner
drinks that are designed
to whet your appetite.
They often have a
bitter element.)

INGREDIENTS

SPIRITS

Gin

The humble G&T's history is closely linked with British history. Soldiers would mix their medicinal quinine with gin in India to fight malaria. After a spell in the 1970s and 1980s out of the spotlight due to the poor quality of mixers and a bad reputation, gin is now most definitely in. Without boring you, gin is basically neutral alcohol flavoured with a wide range of botanicals, herbs and fruits, with the main one being juniper. We all love it mixed with tonic water, a sparkling quinine-based mixer.

Even this most simple of quintessentially British drinks is often ruined by not getting the basics right. Gin, fill with ice, tonic, garnish, done!

Vodka

Arguably the most popular spirit in your cupboard, vodka's neutral flavour makes this a versatile option for cocktails. Recently overshadowed by the gin boom, vodka is definitely back in fashion. Vodka originates from Russia, or Poland (both countries lay claim), possibly as far back as the 900s.

There are so many more highball options than you might think, and believe it or not vodkas can have a hugely different flavour – some are made using potatoes, wheat, rye and even milk!

And no: cranberry is not needed!

Whisky

One of the most complex spirit categories, whisky is probably my desert-island drink. Scotch? If so, what part of Scotland? Japanese? Single malt? Blended? Smokey? Smooth? Whisky can be as personal as wine to find one that you love, but at least there are lots to try.
• A single malt is just a whisky produced and blended at one distillery.
• A blended whisky is a blend of whiskies from multiple distilleries.

Rum

As for other drinks above, rum has multiple categories, with flavours and styles changing completely depending on where it is produced. The main ones you will find at your local supermarket will be:
• Golden – my favourite! Often more complex, golden rums can be great for sipping.
• White – typically the youngest rum in the category, white rum is mostly unaged – they still have plenty of flavour, however, and are great in cocktails.

- Dark – produced from molasses, these rums can be rich and sweet.
- Flavoured/spiced – some are rich with a pineapple flavour, some are light with coconut, some are blended beautifully with spices and vanilla.

🌿 Tequila

Almost everyone has a bad story about tequila. It's not tequila's fault, it's yours, for drinking cheap tequila, and too much!

With white tequila, whether rested or aged, all I recommend is that you chose a good one, and that means 100 per cent blue agave tequila. Most available now are, but some are not.

With all dark spirits, the general rule is that the colour and a lot of the flavour comes from ageing in barrels. Whisky, rum and tequila all start out as white spirits. This means that generally the darker and more aged your spirit, the more flavoursome and complex it will be. Phew!

VERMOUTH

A fortified wine, vermouth is a flavoured, aromatised wine that has had its alcohol content boosted (fortified) by a neutral alcohol and has been flavoured with botanicals, spices and herbs, with wormwood being the key appetite stimulant. It is also a large and diverse category with many different types:
- Red vermouths tend to be richer and sweeter.
- Dry white vermouths tend to be drier and floral.
- White vermouths tend to be sweet and less bitter than red vermouth.
- Rosé vermouths tend to be a little sweeter and fruitier.

COCKTAIL BITTERS

Aromatic cocktail bitters are similar to seasoning with cooking: a drop can bring the drink together and add complexity and balance. Bitters are an aromatic, concentrated infusion of botanicals in an alcohol base and can range from 20 per cent to 50 per cent ABV.

LIQUEURS

A liqueur is a distilled spirit that is then flavoured and sweetened with various fruits, flavours and extracts, and they generally have a lower ABV than most spirits. They can be a great way to flavour cocktails, drunk neat or spritzed with a sparkling wine or soda.

THE COCKTAILS

RUM

DAIQUIRI *BLENDED*

CITRUSY, SWEET/SOUR, BOOZY

The perfect balance of sweet and sour, the Daiquiri originated in Cuba, although the story behind its creation is a little uncertain. Quite possibly it was invented around 1898 by an engineer called Jennings Cox while in the town of Daiquiri. All that matters is that this drink is recognised all over the world. With just three ingredients, it is absolute drink perfection when properly made, and one of my all-time favourites.

INGREDIENTS
50ml white rum
25ml lime juice
25ml sugar syrup *(see page 14)*
4 small ice cubes/45g

ASSEMBLY
1. ***Blend*** all the ingredients for 5-8 seconds, adding the ice to the blender last.
2. ***Pour*** into a coupe glass or a Nick & Nora glass.

GARNISH
1 lime wheel, placed on the rim.

TWIST
• Replace the sugar syrup with pineapple syrup, or add 25ml of pink grapefruit syrup.
• Try with a golden rum for more depth, or a coconut rum.

SPRITZ
Top with rhubarb soda.

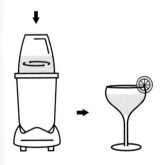

 AVERAGE COST: **£1.26**

MILK AND COOKIES *BLENDED*

SWEET, INDULGENT

Basically, this is milk and cookies for adults with the added kick of espresso. It's a fun alternative to the Espresso Martini on page 37, and a cheeky nod to childhood memories.

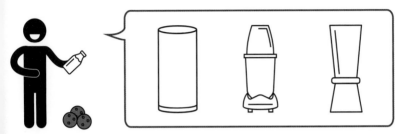

INGREDIENTS
50ml whisky or golden rum
25ml chilled brewed coffee or chilled espresso
90ml milk (whole milk works best)
1 tablespoon/15ml honey
2 small ice cubes/20g

ASSEMBLY
1. *Blend* all the ingredients for 5–8 seconds, adding the ice to the blender last.
2. *Pour* into a Collins glass, or even a mini milk bottle if you have one!

GARNISH
2 chocolate chip cookies.

TWIST
Try with flavoured milks such as chocolate or banana.

AVERAGE COST: **£1.85**

MOJITO *BUILT*

MINTY, REFRESHING

A hugely popular drink originating from the Spanish Armada, the Mojito became known as such in 1800s Havana, Cuba. It's absolutely delicious when properly made – I've probably made more of these than any other cocktail!

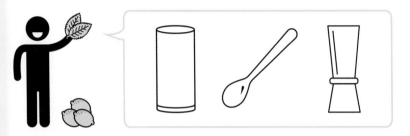

INGREDIENTS
2 stalks fresh mint
50ml white rum
25ml lime juice
4 teaspoons/20ml sugar syrup
  (see page 14)
25ml soda
crushed ice

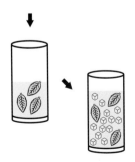

ASSEMBLY
1. *Pick* 5–8 mint leaves, enough for a small handful, and clap them once between your hands.
2. *Add* the mint to a Collins glass.
3. *Add* the remaining ingredients and fill with crushed ice.
4. *Stir* 3–5 times, getting your spoon right to the bottom to move all those mint leaves up through the ice.
5. *Top* with more crushed ice.

GARNISH
1 sprig of mint in the top of the drink, next to a straw.

TWIST
• Try a golden rum for more depth, or even a coconut rum.
• Replace the sugar syrup with a pineapple, lemongrass, or ginger syrup.

SPRITZ
Top with lime soda.

AVERAGE COST: **£1.55**

PIÑA COLADA *BLENDED*

CREAMY, INDULGENT, BOOZY

Yes, we do like! It's possibly my all-time favourite cocktail when made properly. Created in 1952 at the Beachcomber Bar in Puerto Rico, Piña Colada translates into 'strained pineapple' – makes sense! Originally made with Coco Lopez, here we make our own, as it can be difficult to find. This drink sometimes gets a bad rep, but try this recipe and you can thank me later!

INGREDIENTS

50ml coconut rum or white rum
50ml cream of coconut *(see page 15)*
1 tablespoon/15ml lime juice
5 small pineapple chunks (frozen works best)
75ml pineapple juice
4 small ice cubes/45g

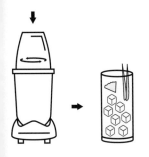

ASSEMBLY

1. ***Blend*** all the ingredients, including the ice, for 10 seconds.
2. ***Pour*** into a highball or wine glass and fill with ice.

GARNISH

1 pineapple wedge, cut and placed on the rim; 2 pineapple leaves, placed together next to the pineapple wedge.

TWIST

• Try adding a handful of raspberries, or even one or two cardamom seeds before blending.
• Using dark, golden rums or a mix can bring out a richer, more complex flavour.
• I love to add 15–25ml of Wray & Nephew Overproof rum to my Piña Colada: it adds an extra bite and has a wonderfully unique flavour.

SPRITZ

Top with ginger beer.

 AVERAGE COST: **£1.61**

DARK AND STORMY *BUILT*

SPICY, BOOZY, SPARKLING

The Dark and Stormy is a delicious and easy-to-make cocktail, popular all over the world. Like a lot of cocktails its history is a bit hazy, but it is a trademarked cocktail, which means this technically has to be made with Gosling's Black Seal rum, although I won't tell if you use another!

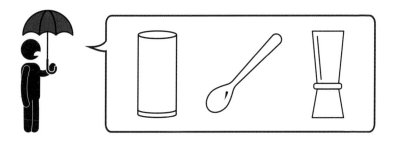

INGREDIENTS
50ml Gosling's Black Seal or premium dark rum
1 teaspoon/5ml lime juice
125ml ginger beer
cubed ice

ASSEMBLY
1. *Add* all the ingredients to a Collins glass and fill with ice.
2. *Stir* 3-5 times.
3. *Add* more ice if needed to fill the glass.

GARNISH
1 lime wheel placed in the top of the drink.

TWIST
• Try replacing some of the ginger beer with pineapple juice or a slice of chilli.
• Add 3-4 drops Angostura bitters.

SPRITZ
Top with pink grapefruit soda.

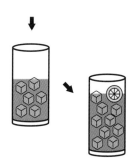

AVERAGE COST: **£2.39**

RUM HIGHBALL *BUILT*

RICH, EFFERVESCENT

White or golden rum works best in a category that has an enormous amount of styles. I'm a huge fan of The Duppy Share blended rum. It hits a great balance between a sipping rum and highly versatile mixing rum.

INGREDIENTS
50ml rum
cubed ice
150ml mixer

ASSEMBLY
1. *Add* the rum to a Collins glass, and fill with cubed ice.
2. Gently *pour* the mixer in.
3. *Add* ice to fill, if needed.

TWISTS & GARNISHES
- Ginger beer, garnished with a lime wedge.
- Elderflower tonic, garnished with an orange wedge.
- Pink grapefruit soda, garnished with a grapefruit wedge.
- Cola, garnished with a lime wheel.

AVERAGE COST: **£2.60**

THE COCKTAILS

VODKA

ESPRESSO MARTINI *BLENDED*

SWEET, INDULGENT

Yes – at home and easily! Legend has it that a famous supermodel walked into a 1980s Soho bar and demanded a drink that would 'wake me up but f**k me up'. The legendary bartender, Dick Bradsell, did just that, mixing fresh espresso with vodka to create this modern classic.

INGREDIENTS

35ml vodka
35ml coffee liqueur such as Kahlúa
4 small ice cubes/45g
35ml chilled espresso, or
  1 teaspoon/5ml granulated
  coffee and **35ml** chilled water

ASSEMBLY

1. *Blend* all the ingredients, except the coffee, for 5–8 seconds, adding the ice to the blender last.

2. *Add* the coffee and switch the blender on for 1–2 seconds – on and straight off. (If you blend the coffee with the drink for the full 10 seconds all you will have is foam. A quick blitz gives the coffee enough aeration to create a wonderfully smooth, foamy finish.)

3. *Pour* into a coupe or Martini glass, leave to settle for up to 90 seconds.

GARNISH

3 espresso beans or a pinch of chocolate powder.

TWIST

• If you like your Espresso Martini a little sweeter, try adding 1 teaspoon/5ml sugar syrup.

• Try replacing the vodka with light rum or even tequila. If you have liqueurs, swap out the coffee liqueur for a hazelnut liqueur or amaretto.

SPRITZ

Top with Clementine and Cinnamon Tonic (by Fever-Tree).

AVERAGE COST: **£1.80**

BLACK AND WHITE RUSSIAN *BUILT*

SWEET, INDULGENT

Ingeniously, these two drinks are named after their appearance, and the fact that vodka is generally associated with Russia. The Black Russian was originally created around 1949. It's unclear when the White Russian was created, but it was very popular in the 1980s and made a comeback after *The Big Lebowski*. Black is without cream, and, yes you've guessed it, White Russian is with cream.

INGREDIENTS
50ml vodka
25ml coffee liqueur
25ml double cream or whole milk (White Russian) (oat and rice milk are great alternatives)
cubed ice

ASSEMBLY
1. *Add* all the ingredients, except the ice, to a rocks glass, with the cream last (if making a White Russian).
2. *Fill* with ice and stir 3–5 times.

GARNISH
Pinch of freshly grated nutmeg, ground cinnamon, ground coffee or even espresso beans.

TWIST
Try adding 1–2 teaspoons caramel or gingerbread syrup; Monin do a great range.

SPRITZ
Top with cola (Black Russian only).

 AVERAGE COST: **£2.39**

VODKA MARTINI *BUILT*

BOOZY, DRY

Possibly, the Vodka Martini is the most famous cocktail on the planet and consumed by the most famous people. Its history is rather fuzzy, but originally it was made with gin and eventually dry vermouth. If you like yours drier, reduce the amount of vermouth. This drink is often the mark of a good bartender: such a simple drink but so easy to get wrong. Dilution is key!

INGREDIENTS
75ml vodka or gin (keep in the freezer)
1 tablespoon/15ml dry vermouth (keep in the fridge)
4 teaspoons/20ml chilled filtered water

ASSEMBLY
1. *Add* all the ingredients to a small carafe or bottle.
2. *Leave* for 2-3 minutes to let the ingredients mix.
3. *Pour* into a coupe or Martini glass.

GARNISH
Lemon zest. Express the zest oils over the drink, wipe around the rim and drop in the drink.

TWIST
• Add 15ml of olive brine for a Dirty Martini, and garnish with olives.
• Adding a couple of drops of orange bitters can elevate the drink.
• The less vermouth you use, the more dry your Martini will be, so try adjusting the amounts to suit your taste.

SPRITZ
Top with orange tonic.

AVERAGE COST: **£2.32**

COSMOPOLITAN *BLENDED*

BOOZY, SWEET/SOUR

Made famous by Carrie Bradshaw and friends, the origin of this super-popular drink is somewhat hazy. More recently it has been perfected by the legendary New York bartender Dale DeGroff, who tweaked the recipe to make it what it is today: one of the iconic modern classics.

INGREDIENTS
40ml citron vodka
25ml Cointreau/triple sec
1 tablespoon/15ml lime juice
2 teaspoons/10ml cranberry juice
4 small ice cubes/45g

ASSEMBLY
1. *Blend* all the ingredients for 5–8 seconds, adding the ice to the blender last.
2. *Pour* into a coupe or Martini glass.

GARNISH
1 large slice of orange zest. Express the zest oils over the drink, wipe around the rim and drop in the drink.

TWIST
Try replacing the vodka with a flavoured gin such as raspberry or pink grapefruit.

SPRITZ
Top with lemon soda.

 AVERAGE COST: **£1.62**

PORNSTAR MARTINI *BLENDED*

FRUITY, SWEET

The phenomenon that is the Pornstar Martini: alcoholic passion fruit and vanilla, with a shot of bubbles. What more do you need? One of the world's most popular drinks, it was created in the early 2000s in London and shows absolutely no sign of going anywhere. It's one of the most popular cocktails in the UK.

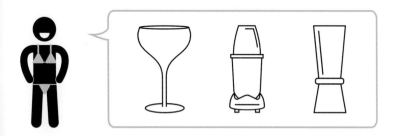

INGREDIENTS
35ml vodka
25ml Passoá passion fruit liqueur
25ml passion fruit purée
1 tablespoon/15ml lime juice
2 teaspoons/10ml vanilla syrup
4 small ice cubes/45g

ASSEMBLY
1. *Blend* all the ingredients for 5-8 seconds, adding the ice to the blender last.
2. *Pour* into a coupe or Martini glass.

GARNISH
• ½ passion fruit, floated on the top of the drink.
• 1 shot glass of Prosecco on the side.

TWIST
• Replace the passion fruit purée with another tropical fruit such as mango.
• Try replacing the vodka with white rum for a fuller flavour.

SPRITZ
Top with Sicilian lemonade or an apple and raspberry juice.

AVERAGE COST: **£2.07**

BLOODY MARY *BLENDED*

BOOZY, RICH, SPICY

One of the world's favourite cocktails, the Bloody Mary is famous for its perceived ability to cure a hangover. Love it or hate it, this drink has surged in popularity, with special attention often given to how outlandish the garnish can be! Its history is disputed, but one claim is that it was invented by Ferdinand Petiot in the famous Harry's Bar in Paris around 1920.

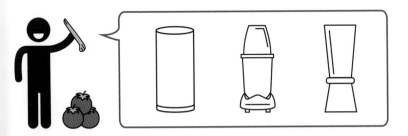

INGREDIENTS
50ml vodka
135ml tomato juice
2 teaspoons/10ml
  Worcestershire sauce
5 dashes of Tabasco
1 pinch of celery salt (or sea salt)
1 pinch of ground black pepper
5ml lemon juice
cubed ice

ASSEMBLY
1. *Blend* all the ingredients, except the ice, for 5–8 seconds.
2. *Pour* into a Collins glass and fill with ice.

GARNISH
• 1 lemon wedge and 1 celery stick or cucumber slice.
• 1 pinch of sea salt and black pepper on the top of the drink.

TWIST
• Replace the vodka with tequila or gin for a more complex flavour.
• Try replacing half the tomato juice for beetroot juice.
• Try adding 5–10ml/1–2 teaspoons olive or jalapeño brine to the mix.

SPRITZ
Top with Bloody Mary Soda (by Double Dutch).

 AVERAGE COST: **£1.44**

CAIPROSKA *BUILT*

CITRUSY, BOOZY

The vodka cousin of the famous Brazilian drink, Caipirinha (see page 121), the Caiproska is such a great, simple summer drink when made well. I remember the first time I saw a bartender in Manchester furiously muddling the ingredients together to help break down the limes and sugar – I was in awe. This method is still widely used, but for ease and consistency at home I use lime juice and sugar syrup.

INGREDIENTS
50ml vodka
25ml lime juice
25ml sugar syrup *(see page 14)*
2 spent lime wedges (left over from juicing)
crushed ice

ASSEMBLY
1. *Add* all the ingredients, except the ice, to a rocks glass.
2. *Fill* with crushed ice.
3. *Stir* 3-5 times with a spoon.
4. *Top* with more crushed ice.

GARNISH
1 lime wedge placed on top.

TWIST
• Try adding the pulp of one passion fruit.
• Try adding 25ml watermelon juice to the mix.

SPRITZ
Top with pink grapefruit soda or mango juice.

 AVERAGE COST: **£1.32**

SGROPPINO *BUILT*

SWEET, SPARKLING

Another magnificent cocktail from Italy. Originally hailing from the Veneto region, you won't see the Sgroppino very often outside Italy, which is a shame. Refreshing, it shouts summer and deliciousness. The first time I had this the Prosecco was floated in the drink, but I think blending just gives it a wonderful creamy texture.

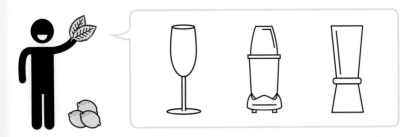

INGREDIENTS
25ml vodka
75ml Prosecco
2 scoops lemon sorbet

ASSEMBLY
1. *Blend* all the ingredients for 5 seconds.
2. *Pour* into a flute glass.

GARNISH
A pinch of grated lemon zest.

TWIST
Try using a citrus gin or limoncello instead of the vodka.

SPRITZ
Replace the Prosecco with rosé Prosecco.

AVERAGE COST: **£1.36**

MOSCOW MULE *BUILT*

SPICY, BOOZY, SPARKLING

The Moscow Mule is a classic vodka-based cocktail that is popular for good reason: it's delicious, refreshing and so easy to make. Just speaking the name of the drink conjures images of the ice-cold copper mug that is the de rigueur vessel for the Moscow Mule.

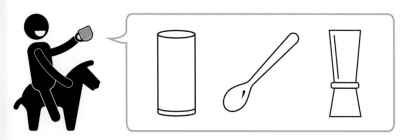

INGREDIENTS
50ml vodka
1 tablespoon/15ml fresh lime juice
125ml ginger beer
cubed ice

ASSEMBLY
1. *Add* all the ingredients, except the ice, to a Collins glass or tumbler.
2. *Fill* the glass with ice.
3. *Stir* 3–5 times with a spoon.
4. *Add* more ice to fill, if needed.

GARNISH
1 lime wheel placed in the top of the drink.

TWIST
Try adding 25ml raspberry purée or swapping the vodka for tequila.

SPRITZ
Top with Sicilian lemonade.

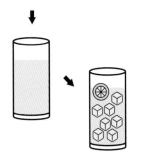

AVERAGE COST: **£1.65**

ELDERFLOWER SPRITZ *BUILT*

GENTLE, SPARKLING

Apple and elderflower: an all-time classic combination. Effervescent and refreshing, the Elderflower Spritz is perfect for an afternoon in the garden with friends.

INGREDIENTS
35ml vodka
75ml Prosecco
50ml cloudy apple juice
1 tablespoon/15ml elderflower cordial
2 teaspoons/10ml lemon juice
cubed ice

ASSEMBLY
1. *Add* all the ingredients to a wine glass or tumbler.
2. Gently tilt the glass, and *fill* with ice.
3. *Stir* 3–5 times with a spoon.

GARNISH
1 cucumber slice and 1 mint sprig placed in the top of the drink.

TWIST
Try using a cucumber-infused gin or a citrus vodka.

SPRITZ
Top with cucumber tonic.

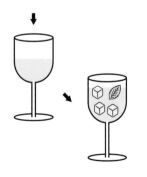

AVERAGE COST: **£1.38**

VODKA HIGHBALL *BUILT*

CLEAN, CRISP

The most versatile spirit in the book, vodka's neutral flavour gives it endless options for flavour combinations. No energy drinks here though, I'm afraid!

INGREDIENTS
50ml vodka
cubed ice
150ml mixer

ASSEMBLY
1. *Add* the vodka to the Collins glass, and fill with cubed ice.
2. Gently *pour* the mixer in.
3. *Add* more ice to fill, if needed.

TWISTS & GARNISHES
• Ginger beer, garnished with a lime wedge.
• Lime soda, garnished with a lime wheel.
• Elderflower tonic, garnished with an orange wedge.
• Raspberry soda, garnished with raspberries and a lime wheel.

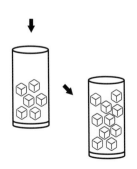

AVERAGE COST: **£1.95**

THE COCKTAILS

WHISKY

OLD FASHIONED *BUILT*

BOOZY, RICH

Come on, you've all made a terrible version of this at home and then given up forever! This is the classic cocktail. Claimed to have been created in Louisville, Kentucky at the Pendennis Club in 1881, this cocktail has stood the test of time. Bourbon or rye, sugar, bitters, dilution. Bourbon is sweeter, whereas rye is a bit spicier and peppery with almost more savoury notes. Some people will demand you still use a sugar cube and try to muddle, but syrup does a better job, instantly blending into your drink.

INGREDIENTS
60ml bourbon or rye whiskey
1-2 teaspoons/5-10ml sugar
syrup, to your taste
(see page 14)
4 dashes of Angostura bitters
cubed ice

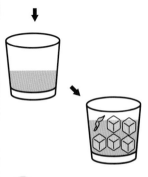

AVERAGE COST: **£1.95**

ASSEMBLY
1. *Add* all the ingredients, except the ice, to a rocks glass, tumbler or Old Fashioned glass.
2. *Fill* the glass with ice, stir for 30-40 seconds with a spoon.
3. *Add* more ice to fill.

GARNISH
1 large slice of orange zest. Express the zest oils over the drink, wipe around the rim and drop in the drink.

TWIST
• Try replacing the bourbon with an aged golden rum, or a reposado or anejo tequila.
• Replace the sugar with 1 teaspoon/5ml maple syrup or agave.
• Add 3 or 4 espresso beans at the beginning of the assembly and leave in the drink; these will impart a wonderfully rich flavour.

SPRITZ
Top with smoky ginger ale.

IRISH COFFEE *BUILT*

HOT, BOOZY

Dating back to 1952, an Irish coffee is such a great drink, but it is one that is often made so badly! The key is getting the cream to float by making sure the sugar is first dissolved in the hot coffee. It's an absolute classic when made right.

INGREDIENTS
35ml Irish whiskey or blended whisky
150ml hot Americano coffee
1 teaspoon/5ml white sugar
1 pinch of freshly grated nutmeg
50ml double cream

ASSEMBLY
1. *Add* all the ingredients, except the cream, to a latte glass or coffee mug.
2. *Stir* with a spoon until the sugar has dissolved.
3. *Whip* the cream a little to aerate it, then slowly pour it on the top of the coffee.

GARNISH
Pinch freshly grated nutmeg over the top of the drink.

TWIST
Try using a golden rum or a liqueur such as Baileys or Frangelico in place of the whisky.

AVERAGE COST: **£1.15**

POP IT LIKE IT'S HOT *BLENDED*

SWEET, INDULGENT

A fun dessert-style drink, Pop it Like it's Hot combines salted caramel, popcorn, coffee and ice cream, plus the added kick of espresso. It was designed for a cocktail class that required one serious drink and one fun drink – you can guess which one this was.

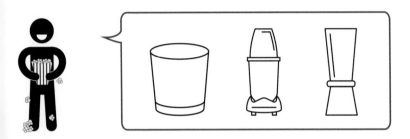

INGREDIENTS
50ml bourbon
90ml milk
25ml chilled brewed coffee or chilled espresso
25ml caramel sauce
2 scoops vanilla ice cream
4 pieces caramel popcorn

ASSEMBLY
1. *Blend* all the ingredients for 5–8 seconds.
2. *Pour* into a rocks glass, tumbler or wine glass.

GARNISH
- Squirty cream.
- 4 popcorn pieces.
- 1 tablespoon/15ml salted caramel drizzle.

TWIST
Try replacing the bourbon with golden rum or a blended whisky.

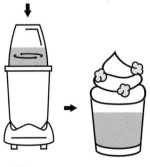

AVERAGE COST: **£1.85**

WHISKEY SOUR *BLENDED*

CITRUSY, SWEET/SOUR, BOOZY

Another golden oldie, the Whiskey Sour was created around 1870. This recipe works with most spirits, Scotch whisky, gin, vodka, rum, bourbon, tequila. If using a liqueur such as amaretto, leave out the sugar. Leave out the egg if you like; this just binds the ingredients and creates a lovely smooth drink – and the famous foam, of course.

INGREDIENTS

50ml bourbon or chosen spirit
25ml lemon juice
4 teaspoons/20ml sugar syrup
  (see page 14)
4 small ice cubes/45g
1 tablespoon/15ml egg white
  (or vegan equivalent)

ASSEMBLY

1. *Blend* all the ingredients, apart from the egg white, for 5-8 seconds, adding the ice to the blender last.
2. *Add* the egg white and switch the blender on for 1-2 seconds – on and straight off. (A quick blitz gives the egg enough aeration to create a wonderfully smooth, foamy drink.)
3. *Pour* into a coupe glass. Leave to settle.

GARNISH

3 or 4 drops of Angostura bitters.

TWIST

• Raspberry syrup is amazing with this drink, or even drop in a small piece of peeled fresh ginger before blending.
• Try replacing the sugar syrup with strawberry, rhubarb or mango syrup.

SPRITZ

Top with Mediterranean Tonic (by Fever-Tree).

AVERAGE COST: **£2.15**

PENICILLIN *BLENDED*

CITRUSY, SWEET/SOUR, BOOZY

The Penicillin cocktail was created in the mid-2000s at New York City's famous Milk & Honey bar. The drink quickly gained a foothold as a modern classic. Technically, this version is a slight twist, as I've added egg white – I think it just elevates the drink and helps to bind the flavours. I love this drink: it's potentially a desert island disc candidate.

INGREDIENTS
50ml blended whisky
2 teaspoons/10ml Islay smoky single malt whisky such as Laphroaig
25ml lemon juice
25ml honey ginger syrup
(see page 14)
4 small ice cubes/45g
1 tablespoon/15ml egg white (or vegan equivalent)

AVERAGE COST: **£2**

ASSEMBLY
1. *Blend* all the ingredients, but without the egg, for 5-10 seconds, adding the ice to the blender last.
2. *Add* the egg white and switch the blender on for 1-2 seconds - on and straight off, or give the container a quick shake. (If you blend the egg with the drink for the full 10 seconds all you will have is foam! A quick blitz gives the egg enough of a blitz to create a wonderfully smooth, foamy drink.)
3. *Pour* into a rocks or Old Fashioned glass and leave to settle.

GARNISH
1 slice fresh ginger placed on the rim.

TWIST
Try replacing the whisky with mezcal or tequila.

SPRITZ
Top with ginger beer.

BOOZY HOT CHOCOLATE *BUILT*

SWEET, BOOZY

This glorious drink reminds me of a winter working in the French Alps. After a hard day out on the slopes, my guests wanted something different from the usual vin chaud. By mixing indulgent hot chocolate with a smooth single malt scotch I created the most popular drink of the season.

INGREDIENTS

200ml hot chocolate
1 large strip of orange zest
2 teaspoons/10ml sugar syrup
  (see page 14)
50ml chosen spirit: whisky,
  cognac and liqueurs work best

ASSEMBLY

1. *Heat* the hot chocolate with the orange zest in a pan. When the hot chocolate is ready, add the syrup and whisky (if using a liqueur such as Baileys or amaretto, leave out the sugar syrup). Stir.
2. *Pour* into a latte glass or coffee mug.

GARNISH

• Aerosol/squirty cream.
• Chocolate powder over the cream.
• Marshmallows dropped in the cream.

TWIST

• Try replacing 15ml of the whisky or rum with an orange liqueur.
• Replace the whisky with Baileys, Frangelico or amaretto.

 AVERAGE COST: **£1.62**

MANHATTAN *BUILT*

BOOZY

One of the iconic drinks, the Manhattan was created around 1880 in New York's Manhattan Club. The recipe is pretty much unchanged since then and is more popular than ever. Use bourbon for a sweeter, smoother flavour, or rye for a spicier, drier taste.

INGREDIENTS

60ml bourbon or rye whiskey
2 tablespoons/30ml sweet vermouth (should be kept in the fridge)
3 dashes of Angostura bitters
2 dashes of orange bitters (optional)
4 teaspoons/20ml chilled filtered water

ASSEMBLY

1. *Add* all the ingredients to a small carafe or bottle.
2. ***Put*** in the fridge until cold; your fridge should be 3-5 degrees Celsius.
3. ***Pour*** into a coupe or Martini glass.

GARNISH

Maraschino cherry dropped in the drink

TWIST

• Try using different sweet vermouths or even ageing your bottle of Manhattan for a week or more. The flavours will settle, combine and subtly change to be slightly more mellow.
• Infuse a batch with cherries.
• Use Scotch whisky for a Rob Roy.

SPRITZ

Top with ginger ale.

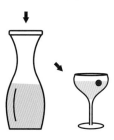

AVERAGE COST: **£2.75**

WHISKY HIGHBALL *BUILT*

RICH, COMPLEX

For such a complicated category, this drink is beautifully simple yet delicious. It works best with a blended whisky or a smooth single malt.

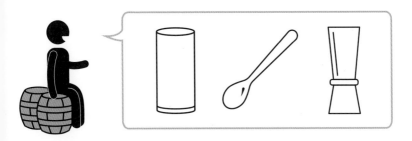

INGREDIENTS
50ml whisky
cubed ice
150ml mixer

ASSEMBLY
1. *Add* the whisky to the Collins glass and fill with cubed ice.
2. Gently ***pour*** in the mixer. Add more ice to fill, if needed.

TWISTS & GARNISHES
• Smoky ginger ale, garnished with a ginger slice and lemon wedge.
• Green tea soda, garnished with a mint sprig.
• Blood orange soda, garnished with an orange wedge.

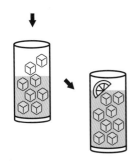

AVERAGE COST: **£2.60**

THE COCKTAILS

GIN

NEGRONI *BUILT*

BITTER, BOOZY

Ah, the Negroni! Out of nowhere, the Negroni became one of the world's best-loved cocktails. Bitter, sweet, dry and delicious, it was created in Florence in 1919 by Count Camillo Negroni (yep!). It's as Italian as pasta, pizza and Gigi Buffon. Still one of my favourites, I love this drink topped with elderflower tonic.

INGREDIENTS
25ml Campari
25ml vermouth
25ml gin
cubed ice

ASSEMBLY
1. *Add* all the ingredients, except the ice, to a rocks glass or tumbler.
2. *Fill* the glass with cubed ice.
3. *Stir* for 10 seconds.
4. *Fill* with more ice, if needed.

GARNISH
1 orange wedge placed on top.

TWIST
• Try replacing the gin with bourbon or rye whiskey for a deeper flavour or with a flavoured gin.
• Pre-batch a bottle of Negroni (see page 17 for how to batch) and try infusing it with fresh strawberries. Remove the fruit after 24 hours. Delicious!

SPRITZ
Top with elderflower or Mediterranean Tonic (by Fever-Tree).

AVERAGE COST: **£1.48**

TOM COLLINS *BUILT*

CITRUSY, SPARKLING

Basically, Tom Collins is a boozy lemonade, first appearing in Jerry Thomas's 1876 cocktail book *The Bon Vivant's Companion*. Originally made with an old style of gin, called Old Tom gin, this drink is very versatile and also works great with vodka, bourbon or rum. It demands that delicate balance between sweet and sour – perfect for a summer afternoon.

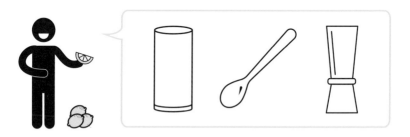

INGREDIENTS
50ml gin
25ml lemon juice
4 teaspoons/20ml sugar syrup
(see page 14)
75ml soda or sparkling water
cubed ice

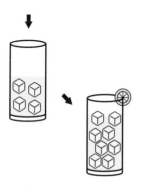

ASSEMBLY
1. *Add* all the ingredients, except the ice, to a Collins glass and fill with ice.
2. *Stir* 3-8 times with a spoon.
3. *Add* more ice to fill the glass, if needed.

GARNISH
1 lemon wheel placed in the top of the drink.

TWIST
• Pink gins and berry vodkas work so well in this drink.
• Replace the sugar syrup with a lychee, lemongrass or strawberry syrup.

SPRITZ
Top with raspberry soda or pineapple juice.

 AVERAGE COST: **£1.46**

BRAMBLE *BLENDED*

TART, FRUITY

Innovative British bartender Dick Bradsell created this modern classic. Bramble is the bush that blackberries grow on, and the drink calls for blackberry liqueur, obviously! If you can't find a blackberry liqueur, try Chambord or a fruit cordial.

INGREDIENTS
50ml gin
25ml lemon juice
1 tablespoon/15ml sugar syrup
  (see page 14)
2 small ice cubes/20g
1 tablespoon/15ml crème de mure

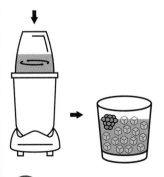

ASSEMBLY
1. *Blend* all the ingredients, except the crème de mure, for 5–8 seconds, adding the ice to the blender last.
2. *Pour* into a rocks glass and fill with crushed ice.
3. *Pour* the crème de mure over the drink.
4. *Top* with more crushed ice.

GARNISH
1 lemon wedge and 1 blackberry placed together on the top of the drink.

TWIST
• Try replacing the gin with white rum.
• Replace the crème de mure with a strawberry or peach liqueur.

SPRITZ
Top with elderflower tonic or an apple and raspberry juice.

AVERAGE COST: **£1.61**

CLOVER CLUB *BLENDED*

CITRUSY, SWEET/SOUR, BOOZY

This Clover Club cocktail can be traced back to the late 1800s and Philadelphia's Bellevue-Stratford Hotel. The pre-Prohibition classic all but disappeared for most of the 20th century, reappearing in recent history to become one of the most popular classics. It's an absolute unsung hero.

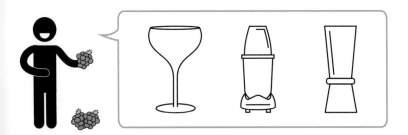

INGREDIENTS
50ml London dry gin
25ml lemon juice
4 teaspoons/20ml raspberry syrup *(see page 14)*
4 small ice cubes/45g
1 tablespoon/15ml egg white (or vegan alternative)

ASSEMBLY
1. *Blend* all the ingredients, except the egg, for 5-8 seconds, adding the ice to the blender last.
2. *Add* the egg white, and switch the blender on for 1-2 seconds – on and straight off. (If you blend the egg with the drink for the full 10 seconds all you will have is foam! A quick blitz gives the egg enough of a blitz to create a wonderfully smooth, foamy drink.)
3. *Pour* into a coupe glass.

GARNISH
3 fresh raspberries skewered on a cocktail stick.

TWIST
Replace the raspberry syrup with a passion fruit or mango syrup.

SPRITZ
Top with ginger ale or soda.

AVERAGE COST: **£1.56**

CLOVER TEA CLUB *BUILT*

REFRESHING, CLEAN

A super fun twist on the classic Clover Club, this drink was a hit back in 2010 when I was working in London. Tea is a great cocktail ingredient, bringing an interesting depth of flavour to the drink. I created this for the drinks menu at a new restaurant opening in Shoreditch; we needed something that customers would love but that we could make really quickly.

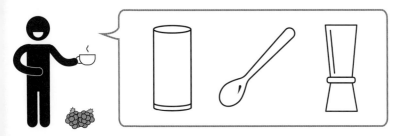

INGREDIENTS

50ml London dry gin
100ml chilled Earl Grey tea
4 teaspoons/20ml lemon juice
4 teaspoons/20ml raspberry
   syrup
cubed ice

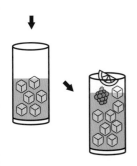

ASSEMBLY

1. *Add* all the ingredients, except the ice, to a Collins glass.
2. *Fill* the glass with cubed ice.
3. *Stir* 3-5 times with a spoon.
4. *Add* more ice to fill, if needed.

GARNISH

1 lemon wedge, and 1 fresh raspberry placed on top.

TWIST

• Try replacing the gin with a raspberry vodka.
• Replace the raspberry syrup with an apple syrup.

SPRITZ

Top with lemonade.

AVERAGE COST: **£1.41**

FRENCH 75 *BLENDED*

SPARKLING, FRESH

The French 75 is named after the fast-firing 75-millimetre field gun that was utilised by the French during World War I. Consisting of gin, fresh lemon juice, sugar and Champagne, the drink is a lot friendlier than the name implies. This is one of the first cocktails I learnt how to make (badly), but now I have perfected it, and it deserves to be consumed more often.

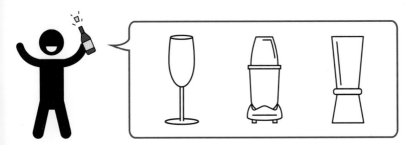

INGREDIENTS
25ml gin
1 tablespoon/15ml lemon juice
1 tablespoon/15ml sugar syrup
    (see page 14)
20g or 2 small cubes of ice
75ml Champagne

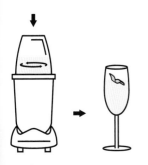

ASSEMBLY
   1. *Blend* all the ingredients, except the Champagne, for 5 seconds, adding the ice to the blender last.
   2. *Pour* into a champagne flute, and slowly top with the Champagne.

GARNISH
   Lemon zest, dropped in.

TWIST
   Try replacing the gin with an elderflower liqueur.

SPRITZ
   Replace the Champagne with a lemon tonic or kombucha such as Royal Flush by Real Kombucha.

 AVERAGE COST: **£2.70**

BEE'S KNEES *BLENDED*

TART, BOOZY

This is a Prohibition-era cocktail: the phrase bee's knees was popular slang used to call something excellent or outstanding. Like most of the best classics, it contains just three ingredients and is so simple.

INGREDIENTS
50ml gin
25ml lemon juice
4 teaspoons/20ml honey syrup
   (see page 14)
4 small ice cubes/45g

ASSEMBLY
   1. *Blend* all the ingredients for 5-8 seconds, adding the ice to the blender last.
   2. *Pour* into a coupe or Martini glass.

GARNISH
   Lemon zest. Express the zest oils over the drink, wipe around the rim and drop in the drink.

TWIST
   Try adding 25ml fresh orange juice.

SPRITZ
   Top with tonic.

 AVERAGE COST: **£1.32**

APEROL SOUR *BLENDED*

BITTERSWEET, SPARKLING

Yes, Aperol can be used in other drinks! Its wonderful sweetness and bitterness pairs perfectly with gin in this twist on the classic Sour. Aperol is often underused in drinks other than the Spritz, but it gives a nice bittersweet flavour and adds a beautiful colour to a drink.

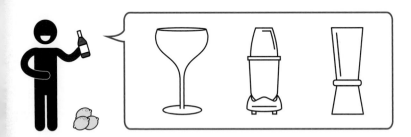

INGREDIENTS
35ml Aperol
25ml London dry gin
25ml lemon juice
1 tablespoon/15ml sugar syrup
(see page 14)
4 small ice cubes/45g
1 tablespoon/15ml egg white
(or vegan equivalent)

ASSEMBLY
1. Blend all the ingredients except the egg for 5-8 seconds, adding the ice to the blender last.
2. Add the egg white and switch the blender on for 1-2 seconds - on and straight off. (If you blend the egg with the drink for the full 10 seconds all you will have is foam! A quick blitz gives the egg enough of a blitz to create a wonderfully smooth, foamy Sour.)
3. Pour into a coupe glass.

GARNISH
1 pinch dried edible petals.

TWIST
Replace the sugar syrup with an orange or pink grapefruit syrup.

SPRITZ
Top with pink grapefruit soda.

 AVERAGE COST: **£1.73**

MARTINEZ *BUILT*

BOOZY

The precursor and cousin to the Martini, or perhaps the lighter sister of the Manhattan, the Martinez is the perfect balance between juniper, floral and sweet flavours. It's possibly my favourite 'straight up' cocktail.

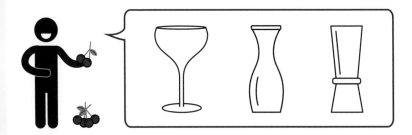

INGREDIENTS
60ml gin (keep in the freezer)
2 tablespoons/30ml sweet vermouth (keep in the fridge)
1 teaspoon/5ml dry cherry liqueur such as Luxardo Maraschino
3 dashes of Angostura bitters
4 teaspoons/20ml chilled filtered water

ASSEMBLY
1. *Add* all the ingredients to a small carafe or bottle.
2. *Leave* for 2–3 minutes to let the ingredients mix.
3. *Pour* into a coupe or Martini glass.

GARNISH
Maraschino cherry, dropped in, or an orange twist.

TWIST
Try replacing the gin with white rum for a deeper flavour, or with an orange gin.

SPRITZ
Top with Mediterranean Tonic (by Fever-Tree).

 AVERAGE COST: **£2.26**

SOUTHSIDE FIZZ *BUILT*

MINTY, REFRESHING

This is pretty much a gin mint julep. The drink can be traced back to 1916, and with the addition of soda it becomes the Southside Fizz. I have lost count of how many I have made at home for friends – now, with this recipe, they can make it for me!

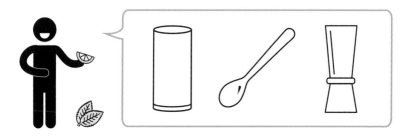

INGREDIENTS
2 sprigs of fresh mint
50ml gin
25ml lemon juice
25ml sugar syrup *(see page 14)*
25ml soda
crushed ice

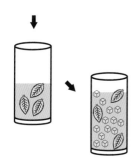

AVERAGE COST: **£1.61**

ASSEMBLY
1. *Pick* 5–8 mint leaves, enough for a small handful, and clap once between your hands, then add to a Collins glass.
2. *Add* the remaining ingredients and fill with crushed ice.
3. *Stir* 3–5 times, getting your spoon right to the bottom to move all those mint leaves up through the ice.
4. *Top* with more crushed ice.

GARNISH
1 mint sprig in the top of the drink, next to a straw.

TWIST
• Replace the sugar syrup with a lemongrass or strawberry syrup.
• Add 2–3 fresh raspberries.

SPRITZ
Top with Mediterranean Tonic (by Fever-Tree).

GIN & TONIC *BUILT*

CRISP, COMPLEX, BOTANICAL

One of the UK's most popular drinks, the G&T is steeped in our history. The juniper-led spirit, mixed with a quinine-based sparkling mixer, is so simple and yet so easily made badly if using the incorrect measures or not enough ice. This drink calls for quality gin, the best mixer, and lots of ice!

INGREDIENTS
50ml gin
cubed ice
150ml mixer

ASSEMBLY
1. *Add* the gin to the Collins glass and fill with cubed ice.
2. *Add* mixer.
3. *Add* more ice to fill, if needed.

TWISTS & GARNISHES
• Premium Indian tonic water, garnished with a lime wedge.
• Mediterranean tonic, garnished with a pink grapefruit wedge.
• Cucumber tonic, garnished with a cucumber slice.
• Aromatic tonic, garnished with a ginger slice.
• Orange tonic, garnished with an orange wedge.

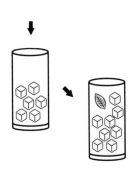

 AVERAGE COST: **£1.95**

THE COCKTAILS

TEQUILA

FROZEN MARGARITA *BLENDED*

EASY DRINKING, SUPER COLD

When summer finally arrives, there is nothing better than trying to recreate that magical, frozen, boozy cocktail you had by the pool on holiday.

INGREDIENTS
50ml white rum or silver tequila
25ml lime juice
25ml sugar syrup *(see page 14)*
50g fresh strawberries
150g ice

ASSEMBLY
1. *Blend* all the ingredients for 10–15 seconds, adding the ice to the blender last. The result should be a nice thick, lava-like consistency.
2. *Pour* into a coupe or Martini glass.

GARNISH
1 lime wedge, placed on top

TWIST
• Replace the tequila with a white rum for a frozen Daiquiri.
• Try replacing the strawberries with mango or watermelon.

SPRITZ
Top with lemonade or watermelon juice.

 AVERAGE COST: **£1.42**

COFFEE & TONIC *BUILT*

BOOZY, SPARKLING

Coffee and tonic is a refreshing way to get your coffee kick, and with the addition of tequila or gin this drink becomes a modern classic. Espresso and tonic has been gaining popularity recently as a grown-up alternative to an iced coffee, while adding tequila elevates it to a serious evening drink.

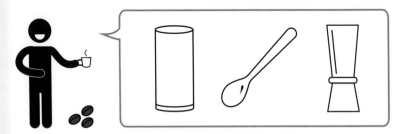

INGREDIENTS
50ml premium silver tequila or gin
35ml chilled brewed coffee or chilled espresso
1 tablespoon/15ml orange syrup
125ml premium tonic
cubed ice

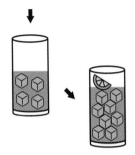

ASSEMBLY
1. *Add* all the ingredients, except the ice, to a Collins glass.
2. *Fill* the glass with cubed ice.
3. *Stir* 3–5 times with a spoon.
4. *Add* more ice to fill, if needed.

GARNISH
1 orange wedge, placed on the top of the drink.

TWIST
Try replacing the orange syrup with vanilla syrup.

SPRITZ
Top with orange tonic.

 AVERAGE COST: **£1.92**

MARGARITA (TOMMY'S) *BLENDED*

CITRUSY, TART, BOOZY

My favourite of all the Margarita variations, this is a more recent iteration of the classic Margarita. I find this tastier, easier and quicker to make, and it doesn't require the addition of a dry orange liqueur such as Cointreau – so there's no need for that orange liqueur to sit on your shelf for the rest of time. High fives all round! It's so simple, and the agave nectar gives the drink a wonderful depth and balance.

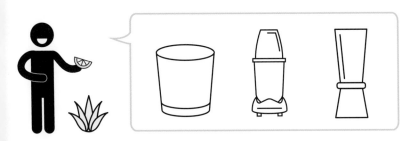

INGREDIENTS
50ml tequila
25ml lime juice
1 tablespoon/15ml agave
   syrup
4 small ice cubes/45g

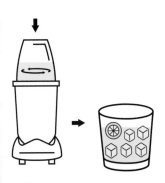

ASSEMBLY
1. *Blend* all the ingredients for 5–10 seconds, adding the ice to the blender last.
2. *Pour* into a rocks glass and fill with ice.

GARNISH
1 lime wheel placed on top.

TWIST
• This version of a Margarita is technically called a Tommy's, so it's already a twist on the classic.
• Try adding 25ml of a nice tart pink grapefruit juice.
• Replace the agave with a chilli syrup.

SPRITZ
Top with lime soda or pineapple juice.

AVERAGE COST: **£1.95**

PINEAPPLE & SAGE MARGARITA *BLENDED*

EASY DRINKING, SUPER COLD

Pineapple and sage just go so well together, and work even better with agave spirits. Fresh pineapple works best, and creates this wonderful, natural sweetness that, combined with the tequila and sage, is a match made in heaven.

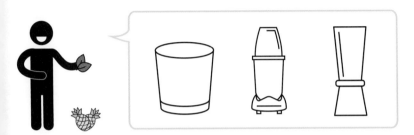

INGREDIENTS
50ml 100% agave silver or reposado tequila
50ml pineapple juice
25ml lime juice
1 tablespoon/15ml agave syrup
1 sage leaf
4 small ice cubes/45g

ASSEMBLY
1. *Blend* all the ingredients for 5-8 seconds, adding the ice to the blender last.
2. *Pour* into a rocks or an Old Fashioned glass and fill with ice.

GARNISH
1 pineapple leaf, and 1 pinch sea salt flakes sprinkled on the leaf.

TWIST
Try replacing the pineapple juice with mango or cloudy apple juice.

SPRITZ
Top with lime soda or kombucha.

AVERAGE COST: **£1.92**

PALOMA *BUILT*

BOOZY, FRUITY, SPARKLING

Meaning 'dove' in Spanish, the Paloma is a Mexican classic. It's a great drink to try if you are new to tequila or just want something long and refreshing. Such an underestimated drink, but this is one of my go-to cocktails when the barbecue is unleashed.

INGREDIENTS

50ml 100% agave silver tequila
100ml pink grapefruit soda
1 tablespoon/15ml fresh lime juice
2 teaspoons/10ml agave syrup
cubed ice

ASSEMBLY

1. *Add* all the ingredients, except the ice, to a Collins glass.
2. *Stir* 3–5 times with a spoon and fill with ice.
3. *Add* more ice to fill the glass, if needed.

GARNISH

Grapefruit wedge, placed on top of the drink.

TWIST

Try adding a large slice of ginger to the drink.

SPRITZ

Top with raspberry soda.

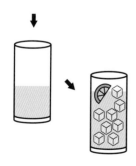

AVERAGE COST: **£2.09**

TEQUILA HIGHBALL *BUILT*

COMPLEX, SMOOTH

There are many great options when it comes to tall, sparkling tequila drinks – its versatile yet complex flavours work great paired with tonics and sodas.

INGREDIENTS
50ml 100% agave silver tequila
cubed ice
150ml mixer

ASSEMBLY
1. *Add* the tequila to a Collins glass, and fill with cubed ice.
2. *Gently* pour in the mixer.
3. *Add* more ice, if needed.

TWISTS & GARNISHES
• Lemon tonic, garnished with a lemon wheel and rosemary sprig.
• Pink grapefruit soda, garnished with a grapefruit wedge.
• Cucumber tonic, garnished with a cucumber slice and strawberry half.
• Premium Indian tonic, garnished with a lime wedge.
• Lime soda, garnished with a lime wheel and orange wedge.

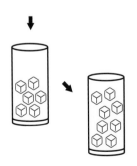

AVERAGE COST: **£2.65**

THE COCKTAILS

WINES, BRANDY AND OTHER SPIRITS

BELLINI *BUILT*

FRUITY, SPARKLING

This elegant drink originates from Harry's Bar in Venice, created in the mid-1900s. Rich and bubbly, it is still a firm favourite, and is simple and delicious.

INGREDIENTS
2 tablespoons/30ml peach purée *(see page 15)*
100ml Prosecco

ASSEMBLY
1. ***Add*** the purée to the flute glass, then slowly pour in the Prosecco.
2. ***Stir*** gently 3–5 times with a spoon.

TWIST
Try replacing the peach with a different purée, such as raspberry or strawberry.

SPRITZ
Replace the Prosecco with a non-alcoholic sparkling wine or kombucha, such as Dry Dragon by Real Kombucha.

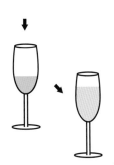

AVERAGE COST: **£1.15**

APEROL SPRITZ *BUILT*

BITTERSWEET, SPARKLING

The unmistakably bright, deep-orange hue of an Aperol Spritz is undoubtedly the sign that summer is here – or that people are trying to will the summer here! Vibrant, fizzy, delicious and very, very popular, this Venetian aperitivo is well over 100 years old but going stronger every day.

INGREDIENTS
50ml Aperol
75ml Prosecco
25ml soda
cubed ice

ASSEMBLY
1. *Add* all the ingredients, except the ice, to a wine glass or tumbler.
2. Gently tilt the glass, and ***fill*** with ice.

GARNISH
1 orange wedge placed on top.

TWIST
Try replacing the Aperol with an elderflower liqueur.

SPRITZ
Top with blood orange soda.

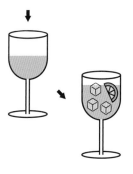

AVERAGE COST: **£1.65**

MIMOSA *BUILT*

LIGHT, EFFERVESCENT

Ah, Christmas Day, the excuse to have a drink first thing, and more often than not a mix of orange juice and sparkling wine! This simple combination has been consumed for centuries in Spain.

INGREDIENTS
75ml orange juice
75ml Prosecco

ASSEMBLY
  1. *Add* the orange juice to the flute glass, then slowly pour in the Prosecco.
  2. *Stir* gently 3–5 times with a spoon.

GARNISH
  No garnish.

TWIST
  • Add more orange juice for a Buck's Fizz or try with a tropical juice.
  • Try adding 1 tablespoon/15ml Aperol.

SPRITZ
  Replace the Prosecco with rhubarb and cardamom soda (by London Essence).

 AVERAGE COST: **£0.77**

CAVA SANGRIA JUG *BUILT*

FRUITY, REFRESHING, SPARKLING

I first tried this drink in Ibiza about five years ago. We'd had an unsuccessful day trying to find a spot on a packed beach with an unhappy young child. Just as we were thinking of giving up and leaving, we sat down, looked at a menu and ordered a jug of Cava Sangria. It was made at the table with lots of fresh fruits, juice and a bottle of Cava – I'll never forget that first taste. We sank the jug, the child magically had a nap, and everything in the world was good.

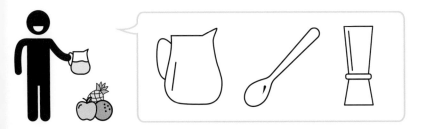

INGREDIENTS
1 bottle chilled Cava
400ml peach purée *(see page 15)*
100ml fresh orange juice
100ml cloudy apple juice
50g mixed frozen berries
5 chunks of fresh pineapple
1 orange, sliced
½ apple, cored and cut into
    small chunks
cubed ice, ice balls or ice blocks

ASSEMBLY
1. *Add* all the ingredients, except the ice, to a jug and stir.
2. *Add* 3 or 4 blocks of ice or ice balls, or fill with ice cubes.

GARNISH
2 mint sprigs placed together.

TWIST
Try adding 50–100ml peach or melon liqueur.

SPRITZ
Replace half or all the Cava with a sparkling grape juice or non-alcoholic sparkling wine.

AVERAGE COST: **£9.50**

WHITE WINE SPRITZ *BUILT*

SPARKLING, DRY

A great way to make your favourite glass of wine more refreshing, a White Wine Spritz is tastier and has a lower ABV.

INGREDIENTS
125ml crisp Sauvignon, Picpoul de Pinet or your favourite white wine
75ml soda or lemonade
cubed ice

ASSEMBLY
1. *Add* the ingredients, except the ice, to a wine glass or tumbler.
2. Gently tilt the glass, and **fill** with ice.

GARNISH
1 lemon wedge.

TWIST
Try replacing the wine with a dry white vermouth, white port or sherry.

SPRITZ
Top with elderflower tonic or kombucha.

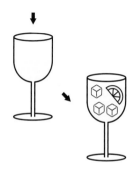

 AVERAGE COST: **£1.62**

RED WINE SPRITZ *BUILT*

SPARKLING, RICH

Such a simple drink, but delicious. I tried this in a small town just outside Barcelona. I thought everyone was drinking Sangria, so I ordered the same. What arrived was even better – a full-bodied Spanish red wine lengthened with tonic – one of my favourite, simple go-to drinks.

INGREDIENTS
125ml Pinotage or similar full-bodied red, or just your favourite will work
75ml premium tonic
cubed ice

ASSEMBLY
1. *Add* the ingredients, except the ice, to a wine glass or tumbler.
2. Gently tilt the glass and *fill* with ice.

GARNISH
1 lemon wedge.

TWIST
Replace the wine with a sweet red vermouth or port.

SPRITZ
Top with lemonade.

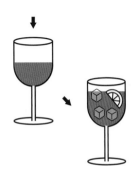

AVERAGE COST: **£1.62**

FROSÉ *BLENDED*

SWEET, GENTLE

Quite a recent cocktail, but extremely popular for obvious reasons, the Frose is fruity, ice cold and slightly boozy. It's a great summer drink, but be careful, because this can be too easy to drink!

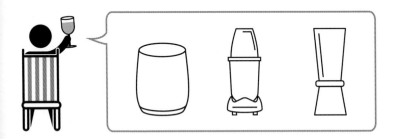

INGREDIENTS

150ml rosé wine, Provence rosé for a drier finish or Zinfandel for a fuller, sweeter drink

50g strawberries (frozen work best)

1 tablespoon/15ml sugar syrup *(see page 14)*

150g ice

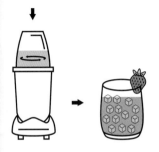

ASSEMBLY

1. *Blend* all the ingredients with the ice for 10 seconds, adding the ice to the blender last.

2. *Pour* into a wine glass or tumbler.

GARNISH

1 strawberry, halved, placed on the rim.

TWIST

• Replace the strawberries with peach, pineapple or raspberries.
• Try replacing the sugar syrup with elderflower cordial.

SPRITZ

Top with lemonade.

 AVERAGE COST: **£1.82**

PISCO SOUR *BLENDED*

CITRUSY, SWEET/SOUR, BOOZY

Peru's famous cocktail, the Pisco Sour, possibly dates back to 1915-20, Pisco being a spirit distilled from grapes. What makes this drink iconic is the addition of Angostura bitters and the use of lime, not lemon, juice.

INGREDIENTS
50ml Pisco
2 tablespoons/30ml lime juice
25ml sugar syrup *(see page 14)*
4 small ice cubes/45g
1 tablespoon/15ml egg white
(or vegan alternative)

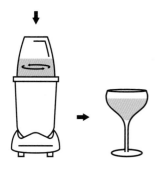

ASSEMBLY
1. Blend all the ingredients, except the egg, for 5-8 seconds, adding the ice to the blender last.
2. Add the egg white and switch the blender on for 1-2 seconds - on and straight off. (If you blend the egg with the drink for the full 10 seconds all you will have is foam, whereas a quick blitz gives the egg enough aeration to create a wonderfully smooth, foamy drink.)
3. Pour into a coupe glass.

GARNISH
3 or 4 drops of Angostura bitters on top of the drink.

TWIST
Try replacing the sugar syrup with a mango or pineapple syrup.

SPRITZ
Top with soda.

AVERAGE COST: **£1.51**

AMERICANO *BUILT*

BITTER, SPARKLING

The precursor to the Negroni, this popular Italian drink originated in 1860s Milan. Refreshing, and with a relatively low ABV, it's perfect to kick off an evening. While I was working in Italy, this was the mid-evening drink of choice.

INGREDIENTS
35ml Campari
35ml sweet vermouth
75ml soda
cubed ice

ASSEMBLY
1. *Add* all the ingredients, except the ice, to a rocks glass or tumbler.
2. *Fill* the glass with cubed ice.
3. *Stir* 3–5 times with a spoon.
4. *Add* more ice to fill, if needed.

GARNISH
1 orange wedge placed on top.

TWIST
Try adding a teaspoon of raspberry or blackberry syrup.

SPRITZ
Top with raspberry soda.

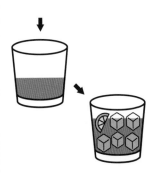

AVERAGE COST: **£1.61**

NEGRONI SBAGLIATO *BUILT*

BITTER, SPARKLING

The story goes that a bartender in Milan got distracted while making a Negroni, and added Prosecco instead of gin. When he tasted his humble error, he realised it actually tasted quite good. Sbagliato means 'mistake' in Italian.

INGREDIENTS
35ml Campari
35ml sweet vermouth
50ml Prosecco
cubed ice

ASSEMBLY
1. *Add* all the ingredients, except the ice, to a rocks glass or tumbler.
2. *Fill* the glass with cubed ice.
3. *Stir* 3-5 times with a spoon.
4. *Add* more ice to fill, if needed.

GARNISH
1 orange wedge or slice.

TWIST
Try replacing the gin with bourbon or rye whiskey for a deeper flavour, or with a flavoured gin such as a pink gin, or citrus gin.

SPRITZ
Top with blood orange soda.

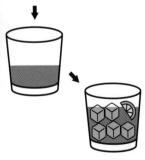

AVERAGE COST: **£1.91**

SOMERSET SOUR *BLENDED*

CITRUSY, SWEET/SOUR, BOOZY

This drink came about after a trip to Somerset and trying a local producer's fantastic cider brandy. It's similar to Calvados – a French apple brandy – but with more of a fresh, pure-apple flavour, and it's absolutely delicious. Mixed with cloudy apple juice, lemon and sugar, this drink is packed full of sweet-and-sour apple goodness.

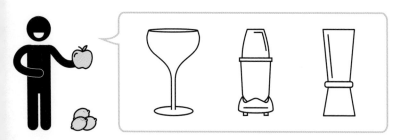

INGREDIENTS
50ml cider brandy
35ml cloudy apple juice
25ml lemon juice
1 tablespoon/15ml sugar syrup
   (see page 14)
4 small ice cubes/45g
1 tablespoon/15ml egg white
   (or vegan equivalent)

ASSEMBLY
   1. *Blend* all the ingredients, except for the egg, for 5–10 seconds, adding the ice to the blender last.
   2. *Add* the egg white and switch the blender on for 1–2 seconds – on and straight off. (A quick blitz gives the egg enough of a blitz to create a wonderfully smooth, foamy Sour.)
   3. *Pour* into a coupe glass.

GARNISH
   1 pinch freeze-dried strawberry powder.

TWIST
   Try replacing the sugar syrup with a raspberry or rosemary syrup.

SPRITZ
   Top with sparkling apple.

 AVERAGE COST: **£1.80**

CAIPIRINHA *BUILT*

CITRUSY, BOOZY

This famous drink is made with Cachaça, the national spirit of Brazil. Mixed with fresh lime and sugar, this super-simple drink can be far too easy to finish. I still remember the first time I tried one in Manchester, not on a beach in Brazil, unfortunately!

INGREDIENTS
50ml Cachaça
25ml lime juice
4 teaspoons/25ml sugar syrup
  (see page 14)
2 spent lime wedges (left over
  from juicing)
crushed ice

ASSEMBLY
1. *Add* all the ingredients to a rocks glass.
2. *Fill* with crushed ice.
3. *Stir* 3–5 times with a spoon.
4. *Top* with more crushed ice.

GARNISH
1 lime wedge, placed on top.

TWIST
• Try adding the pulp from half a passion fruit into the mix.
• Replace the sugar syrup with a mango or peach syrup.

SPRITZ
Top with citrus soda or watermelon juice.

AVERAGE COST: **£1.65**

ICE CREAM COCKTAIL *BLENDED*

SWEET, INDULGENT

Delicious, decadent, and somewhat naughty, this drink is perfect as a post-dinner indulgence while watching your favourite Netflix show. The first time I made this I made a double serving using the last few scoops and served it in the empty ice-cream tub! Salted caramel, cookie dough or vanilla work best. It's great to share.

INGREDIENTS
50ml cognac
2 scoops of ice cream
1 chocolate chip cookie
90ml whole milk
1 tablespoon/15ml syrup – golden, agave or maple
a pinch of freshly grated nutmeg

ASSEMBLY
1. *Blend* all the ingredients for 10 seconds.
2. *Pour* into a rocks glass, tumbler or wine glass.

GARNISH
• Aerosol/squirty cream
• Crumbled chocolate flake

TWIST
Try replacing the cognac with bourbon or golden rum.

 AVERAGE COST: **£1.82**

INDEX

ACKNOWLEDGEMENTS

I'd like to offer full, non-socially distanced thanks to:

My wife Jennifer for believing in me and giving me the support and confidence I needed, as well as being a great drinks taster.

My daughter Marci for giving me inspiration and drive every day to push myself.

The designer Rob Hearn for bringing my ideas to life, and being able to draw up what was inside my head.

CONVERSIONS AND MEASURES

	ml	ounces (oz)
Teaspoon or barspoon	5	1/6
Tablespoon	15	1/2
Shot glass	25/50	1/2
Cup (1cl)	257	8 3/4
Single measure	25	1
Double measure	50	2